LLYFRGELL Y BONT-FA
FFÔN/TEL: 01446 77
BE LIBRA

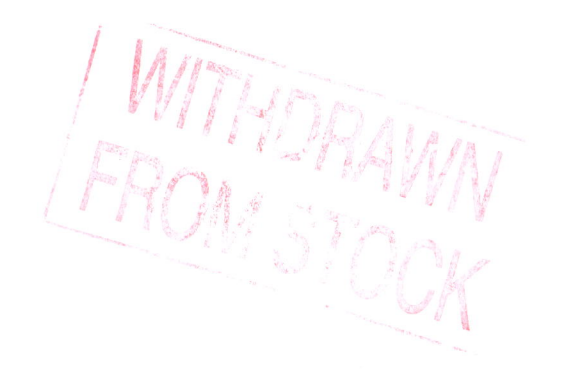

WITHDRAWN FROM STOCK

Book No. 10006093

Smithsonian

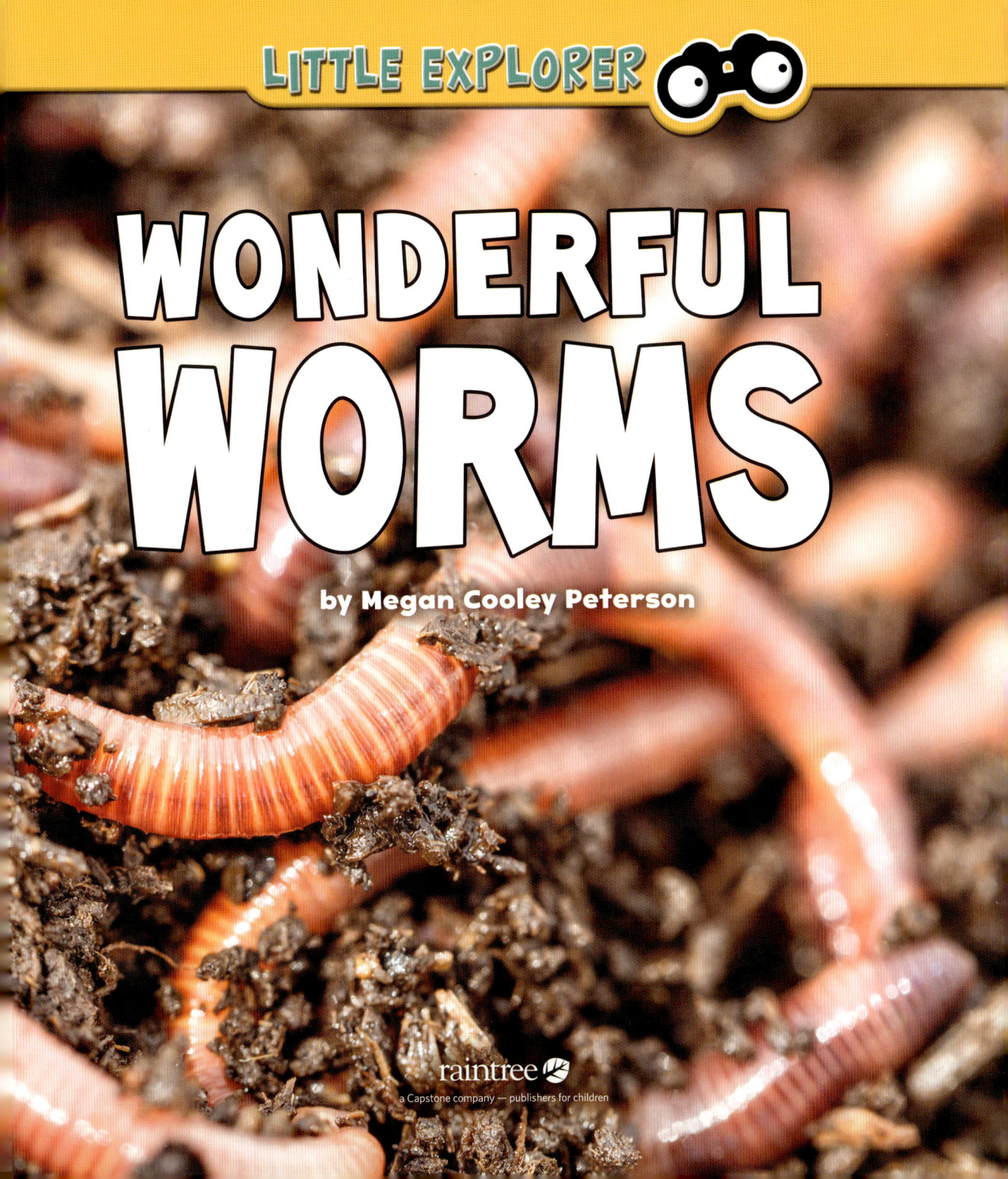

LITTLE EXPLORER

WONDERFUL WORMS

by Megan Cooley Peterson

raintree
a Capstone company — publishers for children

Raintree is an imprint of Capstone Global Library Limited, a company
incorporated in England and Wales having its registered office at 264 Banbury
Road, Oxford, OX2 7DY – Registered company number: 6695582

www.raintree.co.uk
myorders@raintree.co.uk

Text © Capstone Global Library Limited 2021
The moral rights of the proprietor have been asserted.

All rights reserved. No part of this publication may be reproduced in any form or
by any means (including photocopying or storing it in any medium by electronic
means and whether or not transiently or incidentally to some other use of this
publication) without the written permission of the copyright owner, except in
accordance with the provisions of the Copyright, Designs and Patents Act 1988 or
under the terms of a licence issued by the Copyright Licensing Agency, Barnard's
Inn, 86 Fetter Lane, London, EC4A 1EN (www.cla.co.uk). Applications for the
copyright owner's written permission should be addressed to the publisher.

Edited by Abby Huff
Designed by Kyle Grenz
Original illustrations © Capstone Global Library Limited 2021
Picture research by Tracy Cummins
Production by Katy LaVigne
Originated by Capstone Global Library Ltd
Printed and bound in India

978 1 4747 9464 0 (hardback)
978 1 4747 9477 0 (paperback)

British Library Cataloguing in Publication Data
A full catalogue record for this book is available from the British Library.

Acknowledgements
We would like to thank the following for permission to reproduce photographs:
Alamy: blickwinkel, 7 (middle); Nature Picture Library: Nick Upton, 28–29;
Newscom: R. Koenig/picture alliance/blickwinkel, 6–7; Shutterstock: Brian
Lasenby, 16, Chalida Tangjitpakdeesaku, 7 (bottom right), Clark Ukidu, cover,
D. Kucharski K. Kucharska, 8, 22–23, Francesco_Ricciardi, 26, Gerald Robert
Fischer, 12–13, Hans Gert Broeder, 24–25, Hennadii H, 9, Jay Ondreicka, 5 (top
left), junrong, 5 (top right), Levent ALBAS, 17, Maryna Pleshkun, 4–5, Nikolay
Antonov, 1, 2, picturepartners, 7 (bottom left), SARAWUT KUNDEJ, 14, Sebastian
Kaulitzki, 20–21, SIMON SHIM, 10–11, traction, 5 (top middle), vitrolphoto, 18–19

Our very special thanks to Gary Hevel, Public Information Officer (Emeritus),
Entomology Department, at the Smithsonian National Museum of Natural
History. Capstone would also like to thank Kealy Gordon, Product Development
Manager, and the following at Smithsonian Enterprises: Ellen Nanney, Licensing
Manager; Brigid Ferraro, Vice President, Education and Consumer Products; and
Carol LeBlanc, Senior Vice President, Education and Consumer Products.

Every effort has been made to contact copyright holders of material reproduced
in this book. Any omissions will be rectified in subsequent printings if notice is
given to the publisher.

All the internet addresses (URLs) given in this book were valid at the time
of going to press. However, due to the dynamic nature of the internet, some
addresses may have changed, or sites may have changed or ceased to exist since
publication. While the author and publisher regret any inconvenience this may
cause readers, no responsibility for any such changes can be accepted by either
the author or the publisher.

Contents

Make way for worms 4
Earthworms 6
Leeches 10
Bristle worms 12
Roundworms 18
Tapeworms 20
Flukes 22
Marine flatworms 24
Ribbon worms 28

Glossary 30
Comprehension questions 31
Find out more 31
Index 32

Words in **bold** are in the glossary.

Make way for worms

Have you ever dug in the soil? Then you've probably seen a worm! Worms are animals with soft bodies and no backbones. Some are shaped like tubes. Others are flat. Some worms live in the soil. Others live in the water. Some worms even live inside the bodies of people and animals.

More than 50,000 **species** of worms live on Earth. Worms provide food for larger animals such as birds and fish. Some worms add **nutrients** into the soil. The rich soil helps plants to grow.

Is this a worm?

Not all worm-like creatures are worms. Caterpillars turn into butterflies. Grubworms turn into beetles. Silkworms become moths. True worms always stay worms.

caterpillar   grubworm   silkworm

DID YOU KNOW?

Worms come in lots of sizes. Some are metres long. Others are so small you need a microscope to see them.

Earthworms

Number of species: more than 5,000
Found: worldwide
Length: 1 millimetre to 3 metres (0.04 inches to 10 feet)

Have you ever touched an earthworm? Its body is soft and slimy. Earthworms don't have lungs or gills. They breathe through their skin. Earthworms make slime to keep their skin wet. This helps air pass into their skin. Earthworms die if their skin dries. The soil cannot be too dry or too warm.

DID YOU KNOW?

The Gippsland earthworm is the longest earthworm. It lives in Australia. It grows up to 3 m (11 feet) long!

An earthworm's life

Earthworms lay **cocoons** in the soil. More than one baby worm can grow inside a single cocoon. After a few weeks, the baby earthworms hatch. They look like tiny adults. Earthworms live for up to six years.

cocoons

adult earthworm

young earthworms

DID YOU KNOW?

A common earthworm can eat its body weight in food and soil each day.

8

An earthworm is made of many ringed parts called **segments**. Each segment has its own muscles. Tiny **bristles** cover the outside. To move, an earthworm stretches and shortens its body. The bristles grab onto the soil. They help the worm pull itself forward.

Earthworms eat soil. They get nutrients from bits of dead plants in the soil. Then the worms poo out the soil. Earthworm poo makes rich soil, which helps new plants to grow.

An earthworm's body

Earthworms have mouths. They don't have eyes or ears. Special cells on their skin sense light. Earthworms feel sounds with their bodies. Earthworms use their saddles to lay cocoons.

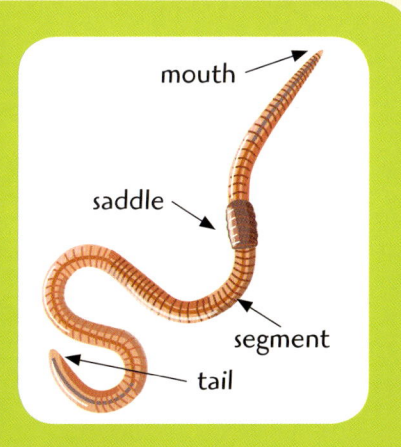

mouth
saddle
segment
tail

Leeches

Number of species: 680
Found: worldwide
Length: 2 to 20 centimetres (0.75 to 8 inches)

Leeches are the vampires of the worm world! They have suckers at each end of their bodies. A leech uses the suckers to hold onto an animal. It bites into the skin. It drinks the animal's blood until it is full. Other leeches eat small animals such as insect **larvae**, and some eat dead plants.

Leeches breathe through their skin. They need to stay wet. Some live on land or in the ocean. Most live in lakes, ponds and rivers.

The tiger leech lives in the wet forests of Southeast Asia.

DID YOU KNOW?
A leech can drink 10 times its weight in blood! Its body gets bigger – like a balloon – as it feeds.

Healing with leeches

Bloodsucking leeches can heal people. Doctors use leeches after they reattach small body parts such as fingers. Doctors place leeches near the wound. The leeches suck up extra blood that gathers under the skin. This helps the tissue heal.

Bristle worms

Number of species: 10,000
Found: oceans worldwide
Length: 0.2 cm to 3 m (0.08 inches to 10 feet)

Bristle worms make their home in the sea. Many look furry! Their bodies are made of segments. Each segment has a pair of leg-like body parts. These parts are covered with bristles. It gives the worm a fuzzy look. Bristle worms use the leg-like body parts to move around. These worms come in many shapes, sizes and colours.

DID YOU KNOW?
The first bristle worms appeared 500 million years ago.

The bristles on a bearded fireworm make it look fuzzy.

A bristle worm's life

Most bristle worms release eggs into the water. The eggs hatch into larvae. Young bristle worms live on their own.

DID YOU KNOW?
The bobbit worm grows up to 3 m (10 feet) long.

Free-moving bristle worms

Some bristle worms swim freely around the ocean. They eat corals, shrimp, clams and other sea animals. Others feed on dead animals and plants. Free-moving bristle worms hide under rocks or in the sand to stay safe from **predators**. Fireworms even have **venom** in their bristles.

The bobbit worm is a sneaky hunter. This bristle worm digs into the sand. It bursts out when fish swim by. Its strong jaws chomp down on its food.

Non-moving bristle worms

Some bristle worms stay in one place. Tube worms make tube-like homes. Some build them out of slime and mud. Others build tubes of hard **minerals**. Tube worms come partway out of their tubes to eat. They quickly tuck back inside when in danger.

DID YOU KNOW?
The colourful Christmas tree worm lives in coral reefs around the world.

Tube worms are also called fan worms and feather duster worms.

Many non-moving bristle worms have feathery **tentacles**. These body parts catch tiny sea animals in the water. They bring the food to the worm's mouth.

Roundworms

Number of species: 25,000–40,000
Found: worldwide
Length: microscopic to 91 cm (3 feet)

Most roundworms live in soil, water or dead plants and animals. But some live inside living animals – including humans! These roundworms are **parasites**. Heartworms are slim, white roundworms. Their larvae grow inside mosquitoes. If an **infected** mosquito bites a dog, the larvae move into the dog. The larvae keep growing. Adult heartworms damage a dog's heart and lungs.

An adult heartworm that has been taken out of a dog

Talking worms

Worms communicate in different ways. Earthworms send messages with touch. Some roundworms use chemicals to "talk". They can tell each other to move away or gather together. Different chemicals send different messages.

DID YOU KNOW?
There are many roundworms living on Earth. Scientists once found 90,000 roundworms inside a single rotting apple.

Tapeworms

Number of species: at least 6,000
Found: worldwide
Length: less than 2.54 cm (1 inch) to 24 m (80 feet)

Tapeworms look like long noodles. These parasites live inside animals and humans. On one end of their body, tapeworms may have a sucker or hooks. These parts grab onto a **host's** intestines. The tapeworm stays there and feeds. It doesn't have a mouth. It soaks up food through its skin.

Tapeworms' long bodies are made of repeating sections. Each section holds eggs. To lay eggs, a section breaks off the tapeworm. Then the eggs hatch.

An illustration of a tapeworm inside an animal's intestines

DID YOU KNOW?

Eating raw and infected meat can give people tapeworms. The beef tapeworm can grow up to 25 m (82 feet) long. Most adult tapeworms are around 5 m (16 feet) long.

Flukes

Number of species: 18,000
Found: worldwide
Length: 0.5 to 10 cm (0.2 to 4 inches)

Flukes are parasites with flat, leaf-shaped bodies. They live in many types of animals. Some flukes even live inside humans. They can make people and animals sick.

Young blood flukes live in ponds or lakes where there are snails. The blood flukes can tell when a person or animal gets in the water. They swim over and dig inside through the skin! Blood flukes swim through a blood vein to the intestines.

An image of a liver fluke taken under a microscope

DID YOU KNOW?

Most flukes have both male and female body parts. They can release thousands of eggs each day. But not all the eggs hatch.

Marine flatworms

Number of species: 3,000
Found: oceans worldwide
Length: 1 to 5 cm (0.4 to 2 inches)

Marine flatworms stand out in a crowd! Their bodies are flat and colourful. They live in the ocean near the seabed. Many make their homes in coral reefs. They blend in with the corals.

The Persian carpet worm looks like a flying carpet. Muscles fill its entire body. The muscles curl up and down to help it swim. This is how all marine flatworms move through the water.

DID YOU KNOW?
Some marine flatworms can live for six months without eating.

A marine flatworm's body

Marine flatworms have simple bodies. They feel with small tentacles. Their eyes sense light and are near the tentacles or around the edge of the body. A marine flatworm has a mouth on its underside.

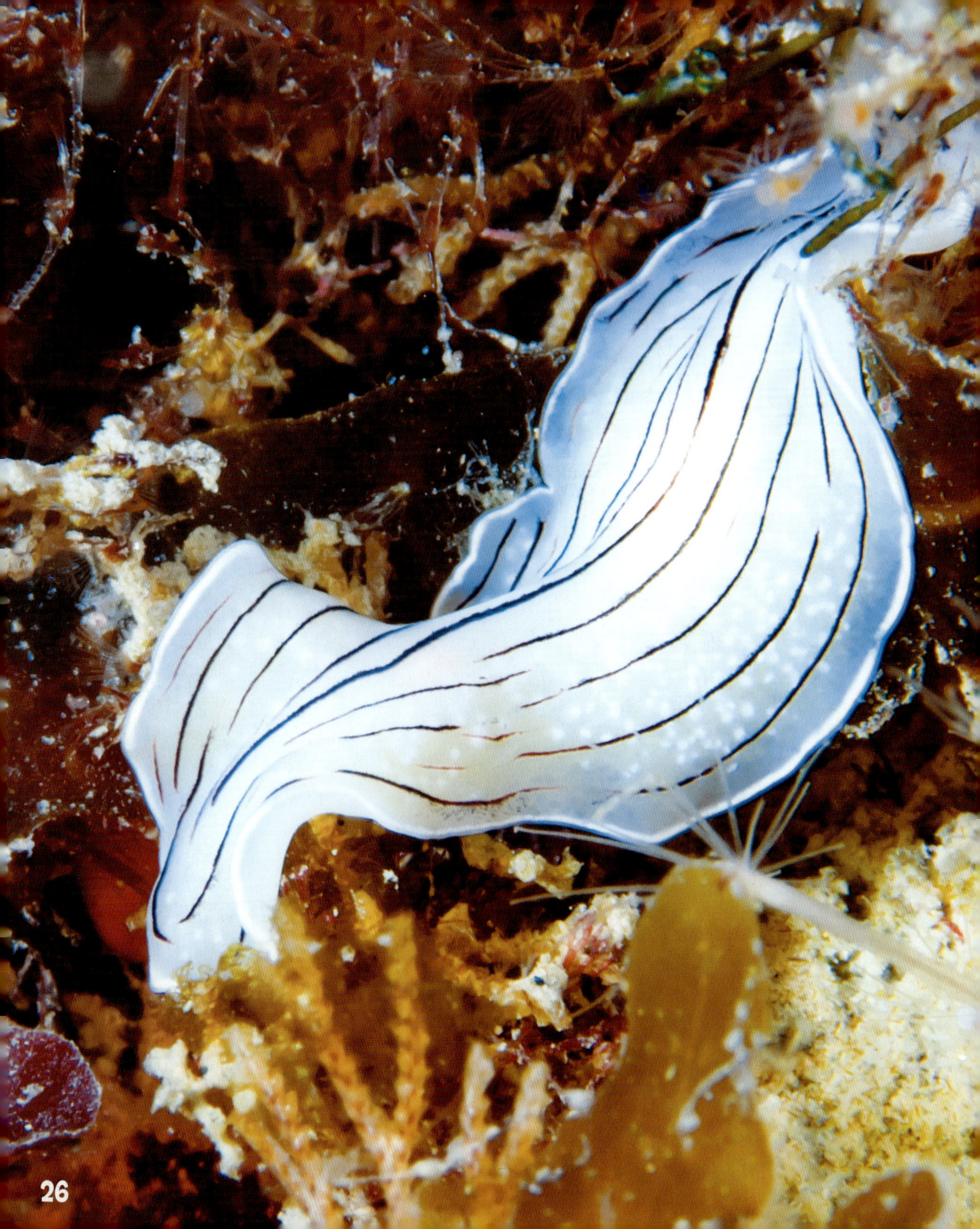

A marine flatworm's mouth is on its underside. To eat, this worm crawls onto its food. A tube-like body part comes out of its mouth. This tube sucks up the food. Marine flatworms eat clams and small animals. They also feed on algae.

Marine flatworms don't poo. Food goes in and out through the mouth. When they've finished eating, they vomit their waste.

DID YOU KNOW?
Most marine flatworms are only about 1 mm (0.04 inches) thick. That's about as thin as a sheet of paper. They can easily tear apart when touched.

Ribbon worms

Number of species: more than 1,000
Found: oceans worldwide
Length: less than 2.54 cm (1 inch) to over 30 m (98 feet)

Ribbon worms don't waste time when catching **prey**. These ocean worms have a **proboscis**. This long tube has a sucker or a spike on the end. Some even let out toxic slime. Ribbon worms shoot the proboscis out of their mouths to snatch prey. Then they swallow their catch whole. Ribbon worms eat molluscs and other worms.

> The bootlace worm may be the longest animal on Earth. Scientists think it may grow up to 60 m (197 feet) long!

DID YOU KNOW?
Some ribbon worms create their own slime. It helps them move through mud.

29

Glossary

bristle short, stiff hair

cocoon small egg-like covering

host living plant or animal that a parasite lives on or in

infected filled with parasites, germs or viruses that can cause illness

larva insect or worm at the stage of development between an egg and an adult

mineral solid found in nature that has a crystal structure

nutrient substance needed by a living thing to stay healthy

parasite animal or plant that lives on or inside another animal or plant and causes harm

predator animal that hunts other animals for food

prey animal hunted by another animal for food

proboscis long, tube-shaped mouthpart

segment one of the ringed parts that makes up the body of some worms

species group of living things that can reproduce with one another

tentacle long, arm-like body part some animals use to touch, grab or smell

venom poisonous liquid produced by some animals

Comprehension questions

1. How do earthworms help their environments?
2. Some worms have segmented bodies. How do these segments help those worms?
3. Many types of worms live in water. How are they different from worms that live on land? How are they the same?

Find out more

Books

Bugs (DK Find out!), DK (DK Children, 2017)

Insects and Spiders: Explore Nature with Fun Facts and Activities (Nature Explorers), DK (DK Children, 2019)

Invertebrates (Animal Classification), Angela Royston (Raintree, 2016)

Website

www.dkfindout.com/uk/animals-and-nature/earthworms-and-leeches/earthworms
Find out about earthworms.

Index

blood 10, 11, 22
bodies 4, 6, 9, 12, 18, 20, 22, 24, 25
breathing 6, 10
bristles 9, 12, 15

caterpillars 5
cocoons 7, 9
communicating 19
coral reefs 16, 24

dogs 18

eating 9, 10, 15, 17, 20, 24, 27, 28
eggs 13, 20, 23
eyes 9, 25

hosts 18, 20, 22

intestines 20, 22

lakes 10, 22
larvae 10, 13, 18
life cycle 7, 13

mouths 9, 17, 25, 27, 28
moving 9, 12, 15, 24, 29

nutrients 4, 9

oceans 10, 12, 15, 24

parasites 4, 18, 20, 22
plants 4, 9, 10, 15, 18
poo 9, 27
predators 4, 15
prey 28
proboscis 28

saddles 9
segments 9, 12
skin 6, 9, 10, 20, 22
slime 6, 16, 28, 29
soil 4, 6, 9, 18
suckers 10, 20, 28

tentacles 17, 25
tubes 4, 16, 27, 28

venom 15

world's longest worms 6, 28